# CONSERVATION
# and
# POLLUTION

## Troll Associates

# CONSERVATION and POLLUTION

by Laurence Santrey

Illustrated by R. Maccabe

Troll Associates

*Library of Congress Cataloging in Publication Data*

Santrey, Laurence.
    Conservation and pollution.

    Summary: Explains how the growth of industry
in modern times has brought about the pollution
of air, water, and land, as well as the depletion
of natural resources, and emphasizes the importance
of conservation.
    1. Pollution—Juvenile literature.  2. Environmental
protection—Juvenile literature.  3. Conservation
of natural resources—Juvenile literature.  [1. Pollution.  2. Environmental protection.  3. Conservation
of natural resources]  I. Maccabe, Richard, ill.
II. Title.
TD176.S26    1985      363.7′3      84-2703
ISBN 0-8167-0260-8 (lib. bdg.)
ISBN 0-8167-0261-6 (pbk.)

Once the Earth's waters ran sparkling
clear. Snow gleamed white at the tops of
rugged mountains. The sky was clear and
the air smelled clean. But over the years,
things have changed. Today, many of our
streams and rivers are not clean. Their
waters are not fit for fish to live in or for
people to drink.

Where a vast forest of tall trees once stood, there are now ugly stumps and bare ground. Gone are the healthy roots that drank in the rains and stopped flood waters from gouging deep gulleys in the land. Even the snow at the top of many mountains is no longer clean and pure. It carries traces of chemicals that pollute the air.

And the vast sky around us has changed, too. Over many large cities there is a haze that hangs like a thin veil.

Air, water, and land all over the world are slowly becoming polluted. Some of this pollution is brought about by nature. Floods wash away fertile soil and leave mud and debris when their polluted waters recede. Periods of drought may dry the soil so much that the wind can blow it away. Forest fires destroy woodlands and fill the air with soot and smoke. And volcanoes pour out flaming lava and choking gases.

But the most harmful pollution is caused by people. When we pollute something, it is spoiled in such a way that it cannot be used safely. Today, our world is suffering from air pollution, water pollution, soil pollution, noise pollution, and solid-waste pollution.

We pollute our air with exhaust fumes from automobile engines and with smoke from factories and homes. We pollute our water by using rivers, lakes, and streams, and even the oceans, as dumps for garbage and chemicals. We pollute the soil with pesticides and chemical fertilizers. We use up the natural resources of the land, destroying precious forests and wildlife.

We strew our waste products over the land, leaving them to pollute the soil, air, and water. We make our daily lives unpleasant with the noise of screeching tires, pounding jackhammers, deafeningly loud music, and the roar of jet engines.

Nobody wants to see the environment spoiled. But there is no easy way to end pollution. The cars, trucks, and planes that fill the air with fumes also help us by bringing the things we need, and by providing us with transportation.

The fertilizers that pollute the soil and waters also help to grow enough food to feed us and people all over the world. Our pesticides may pollute the soil and waters, but they also help us by killing disease-carrying and crop-destroying insects.

14

People are not willing to give up the advantages of modern transportation and the technical advances in industry and farming. Yet something must be done before pollution destroys our world.

Although people have always polluted the environment, pollution was not a serious problem until modern times. Then came the invention of the internal-combustion engine. That opened the door to the widespread growth of industry and modern forms of transportation—and pollution.

Unfortunately, by burning fuels such as gasoline, we do more than power factory machines and move our motor vehicles. The burning of fuel sends millions of tons of gases and particulates into the air. The gases cause severe breathing problems, headaches, and dizziness in people. They also affect the health of animals and damage plant life.

Particulates are tiny bits of liquid or solid matter, such as dust or soot. These particulates cause breathing difficulties, turn the air gray and murky, and even affect our weather.

The most serious problems caused by gases and particulates in the air occur during a thermal inversion. A thermal inversion occurs when a layer of cold air that is close to the ground is held down by a layer of warm air above it. Pollutants that are normally blown away by the wind become trapped in the air near the ground. This leads to higher-than-normal concentrations of air pollutants, which may cause serious illness.

People pollute the water as well as the air. We pollute our waters by pouring wastes into them. Sewage comes from our homes. Industrial wastes come from factories. Pesticides and fertilizers come from farm lands. All of these waste products make our waters unsafe to use.

The sewage from our homes is made up of garbage, human wastes, and household detergents. Human wastes in water cause disease. So most communities remove wastes from sewage before releasing the water into lakes and rivers. The chemicals in detergents, however, remain in the water and cause plants to grow very quickly. They grow so quickly that they choke out most of the other life in the water.

The fertilizers that drain off farm lands into our waters also increase plant growth. The pesticides from farm lands poison fish, shellfish, birds, and the other animals that live in and around the waters. Some of these poisonous chemicals reach people, too, when we drink polluted water or eat something that lived in or drank polluted water.

The most serious water pollution comes from industry. Mines, factories, mills, and power plants pollute the waters with acids, chemicals, radioactive wastes, lead, mercury, and other metals. Industry also pollutes the waters by heating them. This is called thermal pollution. Thermal pollution harms the plant and animal life of these waters.

Industrial oil also pollutes our ocean waters. This oil is the result of spills from tankers and from offshore oil wells. Birds, fish, and other forms of sea life are killed by the thick, gummy liquid. Oil spills also do great harm to the plant life of the ocean, upon which the sea animals depend for survival.

We damage the land by using it thought-lessly and by adding harmful things to it. When a forest is thoughtlessly cut down for lumber, the precious topsoil held in place by tree roots is soon washed or blown away. Soil erosion may also take place when the land is cleared for road and building con-struction, or when farmers wear out the land through poor farming methods.

The pesticides and herbicides that destroy insects and weeds also harm useful organisms in the soil. These organisms help to break down dead plant matter into chemicals that can be reused by growing plants. If this dead matter is not decomposed, or broken down, the soil loses its richness.

The billions of tons of solid waste we throw out every year pollute the land,

water, and air. From the cans and bottles dumped into once-clean streams, to the huge mountains of garbage in our dumps, to the slag heaps near mines and smelting mills, we are burying our land in harmful garbage. These dumps become breeding places for disease-carrying animals and insects. They also foul the waters and send toxic fumes into the air.

The solutions to the problems of pollution are the wise management and the protection of our environment. This is called conservation. We can control air pollution by using fuels that have fewer harmful substances, such as lead, and by installing pollution-control devices on our motor vehicles and factory smokestacks. We can stop the burning of solid wastes that send smoke and particulates into the air. And industry can use devices called scrubbers and filters to keep down the amount of smoke and harmful gases poured into the air we all breathe.

Conservation also means control of water pollution. We can do this by proper treatment of sewage, by cutting down on industrial wastes, and by maintaining high standards of water quality. If the penalties for polluting the water, as well as the air and the land, are great enough, polluters will have to change their ways!

Conservation of the air we breathe, the water we drink, the land that grows our food, and every other part of our environment is important to every living thing on Earth. We must conserve the wildlife that is so critical to the balance of nature. We must conserve the minerals that can never be replaced once they are used up. We must conserve open land for recreation. We must conserve a high quality of life by preventing ear-shattering, nerve-jangling noises.

Conservation is everyone's job. We can all do our share. We can see to it that our community practices conservation, too. Government and industry must also practice good conservation by passing and obeying anti-pollution laws and by using natural resources carefully. The choice is ours. We can destroy the world through waste and neglect and greed. Or we can keep it safe through conservation and care.